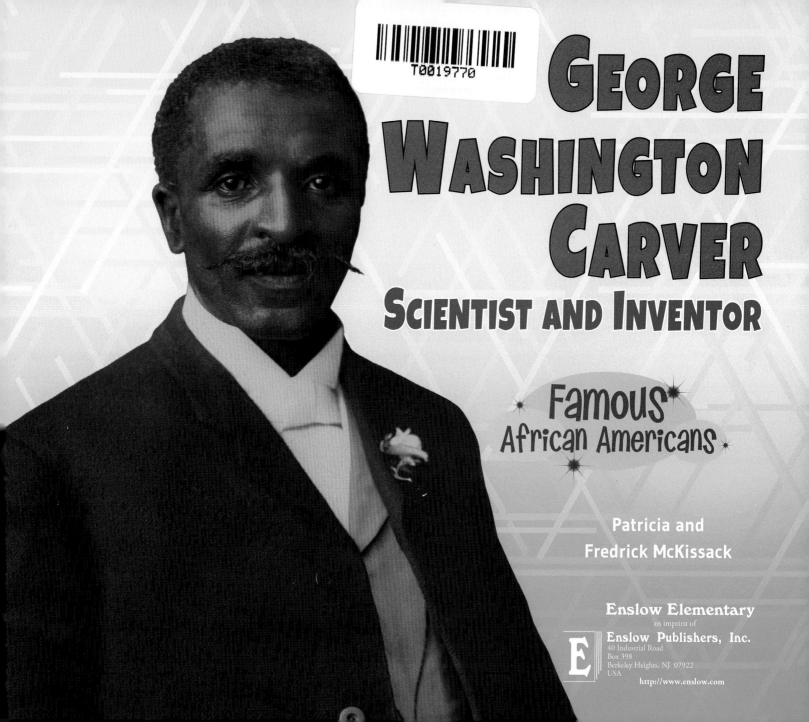

GEORGE WASHINGTON CARVER
SCIENTIST AND INVENTOR

Famous African Americans

Patricia and
Fredrick McKissack

Enslow Elementary
an imprint of
Enslow Publishers, Inc.
40 Industrial Road
Box 398
Berkeley Heights, NJ 07922
USA

http://www.enslow.com

For Margaret Emily Haskins

Enslow Elementary, an imprint of Enslow Publishers, Inc.

Enslow Elementary® is a registered trademark of Enslow Publishers, Inc.

Revised edition of *George Washington Carver: The Peanut Scientist* © 1991.

Library of Congress Cataloging-in-Publication Data

McKissack, Pat, 1944- author.
  George Washington Carver : scientist and inventor / Patricia and Fredrick McKissack. — Revised edition.
    pages cm
    Summary: "A simple biography about George Washington Carver for early readers"—Provided by publisher.
    Includes bibliographical references and index.
    ISBN 978-0-7660-4102-8
    1. Carver, George Washington, 1864?-1943—Juvenile literature.
2. African American agriculturists—Biography—Juvenile literature.
3. Agriculturists—United States—Biography—Juvenile literature.
4. Peanuts—Juvenile literature. I. McKissack, Fredrick, author.
II. Title.
    S417.C3M298 2013
    635'.6596092—dc23
    [B]
                            2012019032

Future Editions:
Paperback ISBN: 978-1-4644-0197-8
EPUB ISBN: 978-1-4645-1110-3
Single-User PDF ISBN: 978-1-4646-1110-0
Multi-User PDF ISBN: 978-0-7660-5739-5

Printed in the United States of America

082012 Lake Book Manufacturing, Inc., Melrose Park, IL

10 9 8 7 6 5 4 3 2 1

Photo Credits: Library of Congress, pp. 1, 4, 10, 13; Moorland-Spingarn Research Center, Hulton Archive/Archive Photos/Getty Images, pp. 3, 20; Photos.com, p. 18.

Illustration Credits: Ned O., pp. 7, 8, 14, 16.

Cover Credits: Library of Congress

Words in **bold** type are are explained in Words to Know on page 22.

Series Consultant:
Russell Adams, PhD
Emeritus Professor
Afro-American Studies
Howard University

CONTENTS

George Washington Carver was born a slave.

CHAPTER 1
STOLEN IN THE NIGHT

Moses and Susan Carver owned a small farm in Diamond Grove, Missouri. They owned one **slave**, Mary. She had two small children, James and George.

One day a neighbor came to warn the Carvers. Slave **raiders** were in the area. Slave raiders stole slaves and sold them again.

The raiders came late that night. They stole Mary and baby George and then rode away.

Moses Carver went after them. He found baby George by the side of the road. He never found Mary.

The Carvers had no children. So they raised James and George as their own. The boys called the Carvers Aunt Susan and Uncle Moses.

George was a sickly boy. His voice was thin and weak. He **stuttered** sometimes when he spoke in a hurry. But he was a happy child who loved plants and animals.

Aunt Susan taught him to read and write. She gave him a Bible. He loved his Bible very much. The boy was always full of questions. He wanted to learn about everything. But the only school for black children was miles away.

It was too far for a little boy to walk each day. George had to wait.

George spent his childhood on a farm. He loved to be around animals and plants.

There were no schools for George where he lived. He left home so he could go to school.

CHAPTER 2
WHY? AND HOW?

When George was about twelve years old, he left the Carvers. He wanted to go to school. He walked to Neosho, Missouri. A family found George sleeping in their barn. They let the boy live with them. George worked and went to Lincoln School.

A few years passed. George learned all he could at Lincoln. He heard about a school in Fort Scott, Kansas. So he moved there. Another family let George live with them. Soon, young Carver was old enough to live on his own. For a while he moved from place to place.

Then he came to a small Kansas town. Another man named George Carver lived there. So George added a "W" to his name. "It is for Washington," he told his friends. George Washington Carver—he liked the sound of his new name.

George (front right) wanted to be an artist when he was a young man. He studied art at school.

George wanted to go to **college**. Not many black men went to college in the 1890s. But George Carver was sure that he would go. He worked hard and saved his money.

At last Carver went to college in Iowa. There he studied what he liked best—plants and farming. Then he went to **Iowa State College** in Ames to study. He **graduated** in 1896. Still, there was much more he wanted to learn.

George Washington Carver would spend the rest of his life asking questions and looking for the answers. He was a **scientist**. And scientists are always asking Why? and How?

CHAPTER 3
TUSKEGEE FARM

George Carver was asked to stay at Iowa State and teach. But Booker T. Washington asked **Professor** Carver to come teach at **Tuskegee Institute** in Alabama.

The all black school was started by Booker T. Washington in 1881. In 1896, Mr. Washington wrote a letter to Professor Carver: "Will you come to Tuskegee to teach?" Carver thought about it. Then he answered: "I am coming."

It was fall 1896 when Professor Carver went to Tuskegee. He had thirteen students. His job was to teach science. But he had no **lab**. This didn't stop him. The class made a lab from things they found.

The students at Tuskegee helped to build their own lab.

Professor Carver taught his students about farming. He had many new ideas about how to grow crops.

The school also had a farm. The soil was poor. The cotton plants were small and weak. Farmers in the South had been growing cotton on the land for many years. Professor Carver said, "The soil needs a rest." He and the class did a project. "We will not plant cotton," he said. "We will plant sweet potatoes." And they did.

The next year they grew **cowpeas**, another kind of vegetable. "The land has to rest," he said.

So the third year they grew cotton again. That cotton **crop** grew bigger and stronger than before. Carver was one of the first scientists to teach **crop rotation**—growing different plants to make the soil better.

The **boll weevil** is a bug that eats cotton plants. In the early 1900s, boll weevils came into the United States from Mexico. Farmers were worried. What could they do? Carver told them to plant **goobers**! Boll weevils don't like goobers.

Professor Carver invited a group of businessmen to dinner. He wanted to show them the many uses of peanuts.

CHAPTER 4
PLANT GOOBERS!

Goobers!

Goober is an old African name for peanut. Slaves brought goobers from Africa. They grew them in small gardens. Goobers were mostly used to feed animals.

Farmers came to Tuskegee from all over the South. Professor Carver told them about his work. What can be done with peanuts? They are only good for hogs, people said. Carver found many ways to use peanuts. His students liked peanut butter best.

Who will buy the peanuts? Professor Carver didn't know. But, as always, he kept looking for answers.

Then an idea came. The quiet professor asked a group of important **businessmen** to have dinner with him. He served them bread, soup, meat, cookies, and ice cream.

Most people did not think peanuts were good food. Professor Carver changed their minds!

They all agreed that the food was good—very good. Then Professor Carver told them: Everything they had eaten had been made with peanuts! What a surprise!

Professor Carver was full of more surprises. He showed the businessmen what they could make from the peanuts. He showed them why they should buy the farmers' peanut crops. What he said made sense. Now the farmers could sell their crops.

It is no surprise that George Washington Carver was called the farmer's best friend.

CHAPTER 5
THE WIZARD OF TUSKEGEE

· ·

George Washington Carver won many **awards**. Henry Ford, who made cars, gave him money to build a new lab. Every day scientists from many countries came to see the "**Wizard** of Tuskegee." Most of the time they found the small, quiet man working.

Professor Carver could have made lots of money. But owning things wasn't important to the great scientist. He owned only one suit. And he walked to his lab every day.

Although he had no wife or children, he was never alone. Tuskegee was home. His students were family. When Professor Carver wasn't working, he enjoyed reading the Bible that Susan Carver had given him long ago.

George Washington Carver and his inventions changed farming forever.

The kind scientist everybody called "Prof" died on January 5, 1943. In 1946 the United States **Congress** named January 5th "George Washington Carver Day." He had given the world 300 ways to use the peanut and 118 ways to use the sweet potato.

President Jimmy Carter, who was a peanut farmer from Georgia, said, "George Washington Carver was a great friend of the American farmer. He was a true genius."

WORDS TO KNOW

award—An honor given to a person for doing something special.

boll weevil—A small bug that kills cotton plants.

businessmen—People who own a company, factory, or store.

college—A school beyond high school.

Congress—Government representatives and senators from each state who form a law making body.

cowpea—A vegetable that is related to the black eyed pea.

crop—The plants a farmer grows during one season.

crop rotation—Ways to rest the soil by not planting a crop on it for several years or by growing different crops.

goobers—An old African name for peanuts.

graduate—To finish all the studies at a school.

institute—A place of learning; a school.

Iowa State College—A college founded in 1858, now called Iowa State University of Science and Technology.

lab—A short name for laboratory. A laboratory is a place where scientists work and study.

president—The leader of a country or group.

professor—A name for a teacher who works at a college.

raiders—Another word for robbers.

scientist—A person who learns about a subject by asking questions and then trying to find answers.

slave—A person who is owned by another. A slave can be bought or sold.

stutter—To stumble over words.

Tuskegee Institute—A college founded in 1881 to teach African American students. It is now called Tuskegee University.

wizard—A person who has great skill, talent, or knowledge.

LEARN MORE

BOOKS

Bolden, Tonya. *George Washington Carver*. New York: Harry N. Abrams, 2008.

Krensky, Stephen. *A Man for All Seasons: The Life of George Washington Carver*. New York: Amistad Press, 2008.

McLoone, Margo. *George Washington Carver*. Mankato, Minn.: Capstone Press, 2006.

WEB SITES

The Great Idea Finder: George Washington Carver
<http://www.ideafinder.com/history/inventors/carver.htm>

The Black Inventor Online Museum: George Washington Carver
<http://www.blackinventor.com/pages/george-washington-carver.html>

INDEX